TULSA CITY-COUNTY LIBRARY

MAR 2023

MRJC

D1716404

For my wee nephews and nieces—
to help remind them of
their Irish blood.

*Special thanks to Rob Bigley
and all my friends who
helped me with this story.*
—N.B.

InterVarsity Press
P.O. Box 1400, Downers Grove, IL 60515-1426
ivpress.com | email@ivpress.com

Text and illustrations ©2023 by Ned Bustard

All rights reserved.
No part of this book may
be reproduced in any form
without written permission
from InterVarsity Press.

InterVarsity Press® is the
publishing division of InterVarsity
Christian Fellowship/USA®.
For more information,
visit intervarsity.org.

Scripture quotations, unless
otherwise noted, are from
The Holy Bible, English Standard Version,
copyright © 2001 by Crossway Bibles,
a division of Good News Publishers.
Used by permission.
All rights reserved.

ISBN 978-1-5140-0724-2 (print)
ISBN 978-1-5140-0725-9 (digital)

Printed in China

**Library of Congress
Cataloging-in-Publication Data**
A catalog record for this book is
available from the Library of Congress.

5 4 3 2 1 | 27 26 25 24 23

Hello, my name is Patrick—
you may have heard my story.
I walked the span of Ireland
to tell of God's great glory.
And with a wee green shamrock
I shared of the Three-in-One:
our God—the blessed mystery—
Father, Spirit, and the Son.

In old Britain I was born
and baptized as a child.
My Pa was faithful to the church,
but me, my heart ran wild.
Then raiders came one dark day—
into slav'ry I was sold!
There I labored for the Irish
in the rain and in the cold.

While serving as a shepherd,
God's grace came down to me.
The holy Dove descended
and gave me faith to see!
God's Spirit was now with me
and all along the way,
I lifted my prayers up to him
a hundred times a day.

But then God sent a vision
while I was fast asleep:
"Back to your home I'll send you—
it's time to leave your sheep.
Look! Your ship is ready!"
I clearly heard God say.
I walked two hundred miles
and found a boat one day.

We sailed off toward my homeland—
seas were rough, the journey long.
But the Lord he brought me safely
to my home where I belong.
My folks rejoiced to see me,
so glad for God's provision.
And to this day I'd still be home,
but for *another* vision . . .

An Irish man came walking
with some letters in his hand.
I opened one he gave to me
and read a strange demand.
"Come walk again among us,"
the Irish folk were crying.
And although their call was desp'rate,
my heart was not complying.

Back to the land of slav'ry?
I could not think of going!
That land was full of evil men
and pagan fires glowing.
They stole me from my parents!
How could that be forgiven?
The only way I could return
was by the strength of heaven.

In grace God did remind me
that forgiveness is a gift.
The holy brothers taught me true
and my heart began to shift.
To the Irish I returned
with a Bible and a bell.
Because God had forgiven me
then I could forgive as well.

To the Irish I returned
to preach of love and grace.
I spoke first to the High King's son
—our Lord he did embrace!
The grateful prince rejoiced because
he had a brand new heart.
He gave a wee old barn to me—
a place our church could start.

I taught God's holy Scriptures
to slaves and to the free.
I said, "Leave your shenanigans
and seek the One-in-Three!"

I saw the Spirit moving
all across the Emerald Isle.
It wasn't luck—it was God's grace,
and that always makes me smile!

The Irish love good stories,
and tales both big and small,
where bad men become foxes
or short men become tall.
There is a famous legend
—you still hear of it today—
I gathered all the serpents up
and cast them in the bay!

Another wondrous story
that the Irish tell of me:
I found a naughty giant
under rocks down by the sea.
The giant was repentant,
the storytellers say,
so I told him of the love of God
and baptized him that day.

Sure, some stories stretch the truth
but I'll say without a doubt,
the passion for those pagan gods
has nearly all burnt out!
The druids, too, they're all gone—
their strange fires died away.
The Spirit now is burning bright
for follow'rs of the Way.

It is a joy to shepherd
and to serve my Irish flock.
I tell them about forgiveness
found in Christ, our mighty rock.
I set up schools throughout the land
that offer godly teaching,
and I founded many churches
for worship and for preaching.

To every ear that hears me
I preach Christ, and Christ alone:
Christ above me, Christ within me,
Christ on his golden throne.
And by the strength of heaven
I will love and I'll forgive—
and I'll belong to Jesus
for as long as I shall live!